HOLOGRAPHIC
REALITY

POEMS OF AN ECLECTIC LIFE

HOLOGRAPHIC REALITY
POEMS OF AN ECLECTIC LIFE
Copyright © 2024 Seretta Martin

Library of Congress Cataloguing-in-Publication Data
Name: Martin, Seretta, author
Title: Holographic Reality / Poems of an Eclectic Life
Description: San Diego, California: Blue Vortex Publishers
Identifiers: LLCN 2022916883 (paperback)
ISBN: 978-0-9726210-4-5
Subjects: LCSH: Martin, Seretta – Poetry: History, Art, Surrealism, Fantasy, Dreams, Science, Pandemic, War, Love, Travel, Heliography, Out-of-Body experiences, Haiku and Haibun.

Editors: Fred Longworth & Nancy Sandweiss
Technical Editor & Cover design: Clifton King
Cover Photo: Seretta Martin

Published by Blue Vortex Publishers, San Diego, California
Printed in the United States
First Edition — 10 0 8 7 6 5 4 3 2 1

Praise for the author's books

"Seretta Martin is a poet who is able to bring together lyric impulse and wisdom of experience in a way that is inspiring, entertaining and consoling. Her eye for image and detail is spellbinding. Read her haiku and you will find yourself thinking that a moment stops. Her imagination, especially in her longer sequences, captivates us. This is a poet whose work will find many readers."

ILYA KAMINSKY, author, translator, editor, professor,
Deaf Republic, Dancing in Odessa

"Let early morning rain clatter up flights of stairs," Seretta Martin writes. Her poetry breaks open doors, finds shadows in corners, uncovers family secrets, throws back the sheets so lovers can lie uncovered. It is a poetry of the stories we tried to forget, the stories that form us. "Is there a soul?" she writes, "who doesn't dream of home?

KATE GALE, managing editor; Red Hen Press, author,
Under a Neon Sun, The Loneliest Girl, Echo Light, The Goldilocks Zone

"Seretta Martin's collection of poems, **Foreign Dust, Familiar Rain** dance with her surreal and enigmatic drawings. Her cover of green vines surrounds a classical statue of a woman who gazes adoringly at something beyond our view. That "something" is revealed within each poem. Steal a moment and step into just one of her poems. Then watch the world around you and within you change, quietly, imperceptibly. You will be so glad you did!"

~KATE CALLAGY

"A wonderful collection of poems in different styles, lightly and pleasantly embellished by the author's own drawings, *Foreign Dust, Familiar Rain* is a fine mix of the foreign and the familiar. From the haunting "Monarch," described as a true story at Ground Zero to the playful "Cosmic Latte," there is truth in each poem. No extra words, no wasted effort. *Reflections in the Pond* is my favorite, as memories or her feelings battle one another. It ends, "petals floated in the pond where summer seemed to love itself as if it claimed all the seasons." And then, indented and italicized, "No, not all of them." Sweet… I was immediately taken by the book's cover, and it bespoke the high quality of the book's production."

~ SIMON MAYESKI

HOLOGRAPHIC
REALITY

POEMS OF AN ECLECTIC LIFE

———

Seretta Martin

BLUE VORTEX PUBLISHERS

Poetry heals the wounds inflicted by reason

~Novalis, German Romantic poet

for Marion, Una, Litta, Helen, Betsey, Roz,
and you, my reader

TABLE OF CONTENTS

RARE BLUE MOON

GHOST TWIGS

BLOOD MUSIC

Live the questions now. Perhaps then, someday far in the
future, you will gradually, without even noticing it, live
your way into the answer.

–Rainer Maria Rilke, *Letters to a Young Poet*

INTRODUCTION

Seretta Martin's poetry is distinguished by its clarity, intelligent
simplicity, and to quote Ilya Kaminsky, "Her eye for detail and
image is spellbinding." This is poetry of engagement — original,
interesting, and stimulating. Extended metaphors, precise
language, and pacing characterize her lyrical style.

Holographic Reality has poems that are like movie moments, a
quality inherited from her study of cinema and visual art. Many
of them are holograms — life's impermanent moments illuminated
by 3-D focus. The piece, "Abductor" describes a surreal
holographic out-of- body experience where she saw "the light"
beyond this lifetime but made the decision to stay with humanity
rather than transcend. Other poems address themes of dreams and
unsettling imaginative alternate realities.

"It is a poetry of the stories we tried to forget, the stories that
inform us," (Kate Gale) This is true in a series of poems that take
place in Connecticut where she lived in her twenties — those
difficult and impressionable years which Seretta considers "the
best and the worst of times."

You will witness poems of love, compassion, art, loss, grief, aging,
mortality, war, apocalyptic visions, physics, and ecology, as well as
important societal issues like the pandemic of this century. Some
poems are playful, others she refers to as "portrait poems"
showing the vulnerability and resilience of herself and others.
Her poetic ambiguities serve as a powerful tool for creativity, and
reflection. By not spelling out everything, space is left for the
reader to enter a poem and contemplate the meaning.

Her innovative writing in this book and others takes the shape of free verse, sonnet and other traditional forms. Haiku, senryu, monoku and haibun, reflect her affinity for Chinese and Japanese aesthetics, especially Zen. As a visual artist her haiku also express a love for minimalism. You can see how she has been inspired by Ruth Stone's accuracy, strangeness and humor, and Charles Simic's surrealism, wit, and irony.

Earlier influences include Neruda, Rumi, Hart Crane, Robert Frost and more recently, Linda Pastan. She has always admired Ray Bradbury, George Orwell, Alfred Hitchcock, Salvador Dali and Maurits Cornelis Escher.

Each chapter begins with a quote by Novalis, Rainer Maria Rilke, Arthur Conan Doyle, Allen Ginsberg, Jack Kerouac, John Lennon, Alfred Hitchcock, Woody Allen, Willian Burroughs, William Stafford, George Orwell, Charles Wright, Yehuda Amichai and Seretta's best friend and poetry mentor, Una Nichols Hynum.

~S.M.D.

The mind is holographic in nature and exists outside of the body, distributed across the infinite sub-quantum infrastructure of the universe…sub-quantum physics provides a rational framework which explains such so-called "paranormal" phenomena as Precognition, Psychometry, Telepathy, Reincarnation, Mediumship, Out-Of-Body Experience, and The Akashic Records…

~Louis Malklaka, author of *Holographic Sub-Quantum Mind*

HOLOGRAPHIC
REALITY

POEMS OF AN ECLECTIC LIFE

Time is unbuttoned, the train
clicking like spoons…

no yesterday

no tomorrow

only the journey…

~Una Nichols Hynum, *Night Train*

The Weight of Things Seen

If a window bears the weight of its view,
does what young oaks witness
measure lighter than the stately pine
looming with its grand crown—
the watchtower for fire, forest, and eagle?

What does the fleeting sight of a flying
squirrel weigh — does the sum of their solitude
and solid authority make a mass of rocks
heavier — would the rim-light on a spider's
thread weigh a fraction of a dewdrop?

Maybe it doesn't matter —
a flood may wash through, shattering
a window to a fractured scene
too finite to measure, fragments adrift
in a raging rush of water — the sun

contemplates glass, the window
a memory of its view
gives a glimpse of possibilities
nearly weightless when embraced by all
outside the floating frame.

Between Stops

You travel backwards
on a night train, wheels grinding
beneath the seat, light races, silhouettes
blur the parentheses of spruce trees
in a place you will never stop to visit.
The whistle leans into the absence of light
along this stretch of miles between
your previous and the next stop.
Is there nothing for you in between?

The coach slides to a stop. Outside
a phone booth glows, lit by September's moon—
the phone dangles off its hook.

---

across this river
a train whistle at noon
ghost conductor

shooting star
looking away
at the right time

old foundation
with a canyon view
wind lives here

abalone moon
the sidewalk drawing
signed by a snail

in oak branches
visiting the moon
a white owl

TRANSFIGURED

Once you eliminate the impossible, whatever remains,
however improbable, must be the truth

Arthur Conan Doyle

Sanding Fingertips

a nod to Ray Bradbury

I took the train with no passengers, driven
by a conductor with swollen dots on his fingers.

Arriving in Seezaira, I stepped down from the platform,
zest of cinnabar overcame me. Someone approached from

behind, cold hands tied a rough blindfold over my eyes,
led me through a riddle of cobbled streets.

Counting my breath like breadcrumbs, I could have told you
how many sighs it took to get from the station to my hotel.

The porter said, *Here people thrive on all but one
of their senses and speaking of that absence is forbidden.*

At a wooden table scarred by knifes a crowd
shunned the musk-soil aroma of noxious mushrooms

and savored warm purple potatoes. An old woman's
tongue raked over the endings of medieval tales.

In Seezaira, village of the blind, when bells tolled
people sang, performing a ritual sanding of fingertips.

One Act

What we miss, our mind fills in

Had I not heard of an epic event
I would have been baffled and anxious
trying to decipher voices in the obscure haze
of a crop-dusted cornfield blown bare.

Scarcely able to capture a word here and there
I felt the thud of warriors shake the ground, saw
a flash of crimson, heard spine-chilling screams
and laughter. I couldn't see the audience through
smoke so thick you could cut it with a saber.

Earlier, had I not seen thespians arrive in battle regalia
I wouldn't have known their uniforms, except
for a glimpse of metal when the moon appeared
and escaped behind an arena of explosions.

And at the end of the drama when I saw
an actress crossing the field headed back to her trailer
I asked,
     Why no lights? What was the plot?
  Was it the Middle Ages or current times? Who won?

…and like the sarcastic Red Queen, she snapped,
     Had you been paying attention, you
     wouldn't ask. Use your imagination!

Silent Film Theater

Decades of empty theater seats, a baby grand in the alcove
layered with a patina of white pigeon dung—its keyboard,
a progression of dry notes. We are given palette knives and
tin buckets. If not for us, there'd be only spiders draping
their webs between moth-eaten red velvet curtains, mice
scurrying amid rows of shadows, a faint aroma-memory
of popcorn. Any minute, I expect to see, on the frayed
silver screen, *Tess of Storm County* "America's sweetheart,"
Mary Pickford, fluttering her eyelids, flipping ringlets,
flouncing sheer petticoats to the classical music of her era.
A chair creaks. A pigeon coos in the wings.

    all-day suckers
    our lips chapped from kissing
    in the balcony

Silver Screen

The ocean
an endless reel
films itself —
waves dashing
frame by frame
moving the sunset to shore.
Time, an endless editor—
clips summer's drama
families
    lovers
        and extras
Liquid colors—
sea birds
track my steps
waves meet
desert air
florescent sun
flickers
in pink-rim clouds
    sand dreams
        you are here.

At the Comic-Con of the Future

…a roulette wheel lands on a *Trip to the Mars*

Thousands from around the globe
take the spin — red or black, odd, or even—
    A ball whirls opposite the tilted track,
    eventually loses momentum and falls — a win.

At the admission gate, an android scanner
like a slap-stick cartoon character
self-adjusts to the level of each attendee,
reads iris after iris.

Wrinkled grown-ups, who, like kids
crave instant flash, dash of color,
the clamor-boom-crash of action-packed videos,
bask in the glow of giant plasma screens.

Over there a Superhero poses, flexes biceps.
His long-legged alien girlfriend in black
fishnets, adjusts her thong, poses for a photo.
Children imitate as if their future depends on it.

      glistening in a city gutter
      Morticia's black fingernail
      summer thunder

Listen Baby-Boomers

It's time! Fling back the sheets,
get your parents out of bed,
they've been warehoused too long.
I know, my dad is one of them.
Paint those drab rehab walls,
hang paintings, paisley curtains.

Let there be a garden room, light,
cirrus clouds, butterflies.
Let them have a bubble machine,
a silver ballroom, Dixie and Swing,
Crank up the karaoke, *Sweet Georgia Brown.*
Bring on the trumpets.

And for insomniacs —
give them an all-night theater wing,
popcorn for those who can chew,
bonbons for those who can't.

———————————

reflections —
the curve of her hip
in his coffee cup

Ode to Marc Chagall

after a retrospective exhibit, San Francisco

After your love Bella died, her absence
saturated your pallet, staining
your paintings with grief.

Lovers in crimson, no longer floated defying
gravity, nudes who once embodied light,
now victims — their skin a mournful mauve.

Even your playful animals oozed
matador red, the rooster grew enormous
glaring at lovers with one sad eye.

In the corner of a canvas a carnival faded
to a melancholy vignette, a somber, dizzy-
hearted jester turned no stunts, strummed a dirge.

The wedding couple, too dazed to dance,
froze, muted in the weight of lost days.

Your bride held a wire-stemmed bouquet,
buds never to open amid wilted leaves
the scent of mausoleum musk, and you—

painted a tragic blue, and the yellow,
"elusive" bull art critics don't understand
turned to embrace your Bella.

David Shivers

after Michelangelo's David

After hours. I sneak into the museum
for a rendezvous with David,
slide onto the pedestal, stretch before him.
Eyes closed I listen, hear a toccata.

I feel the nude coolness in his solid curves,
the contour of his arms. Neck tendons
strained, David leans toward me with
his vulnerable left side. In my palms I

cup his jaw. His lush curls turn in
on themselves like private whispers.
I smell olive on his cheek as his lips
break centuries of silence.

Photo I Missed in Spain

The weight of years in black

On a quiet cobbled street in Madrid
late afternoon sun sheds Rembrandt lighting
on the nana's lined face, skirt flowing long
around her swollen ankles.

A photo opportunity.

She stands holding a toddler's hand.
I see the contrast between nana's
black smock and the child's pink pinafore —
a classic image of youth and old age.

Suddenly, the toddler breaks loose
running away from nana like a gleeful puppy.
Too crippled to run, Nana, hobbles forward.

I peer through the lens, but like paint drying
before the masterpiece is complete,
my camera jams —

The Purse, Nome Alaska

In the Gold Rush Tavern, I withdrew when a dim-eyed man
rushed up to a young woman sitting on the stool next to me.
He demanded something. She reached into her jeans pocket,
pulled out a small purse, and handed it to him. Was this a
shakedown? No, something else. He didn't open it.
A plaintive open-mouthed smile smoothed across his round
child-like face — eyes pooled as he cupped the purse in both
hands, fingering rows of beads — the pattern finely stitched
on leather in red, yellow and blue. The woman sipped her
beer and said nothing, a sled dog calm by her side. When the
man looked up at her, words stumbled from his mouth like
shattered glass, *Thaaank youuu.* Carefully, he handed her the
purse as if returning a fledgling to its nest. Giving him a nod
of compassion, she slid the purse back into her pocket. After
he limped back to his bar stool she said,

> *My cousin asks to see it every time —*
> *the last purse his mother made.*

———————————

autumn in Alaska
lining every rooftop
moose antlers

Found in Alaska

Consider the enormous reach
of a Sitka spruce, the vast range of the Yukon,
aurora borealis sweeping the sky.

In Alaska on a two-lane road, we round a curve
to a waterfall so close to the berm I

roll down my window, feel cool spray,
wonder if the falls freeze over in winter
forming an ice-sculpture of waves between trees.

At a roadside gift shop, I find my childhood
fascination with the prehistoric — a miniature
mastodon one inch tall, carved of ivory by a local artist.

I imagine the grand creature's weight —
enough to crush me with one step as it roamed
swamps and forests grazing on conifers and grass.

Yet, this mastodon's tooth-pick-thin tusks
could readily snap in an able artist's hands.

Later, scarfed and swaddled in my carry-on,
the mastodon will travel home to a curio case
to reside with a fetish of horse, eagle, and rabbit.

Consider the enormous and small —
you and I, fragile and fleeting.

Old Gentleman of Raahe, Finland, Museum

In a glass display case
this cone-head with round
porthole eyes and mouth
could be the inspiration
for a creature in an early
B-rated space movie —
the old gent's suit of metallic cloth,
now cracked and dull,
salted with ocean patina.
If you were to climb inside
this 19th century diving suit,
the oldest known to man,
would you gasp for air,
feel the ocean
seep through seams,
hear the echo of seagulls,
and the song of whales
transporting you through time
to a memory of drowning?

---

dreaming of a woman
trapped underwater
my leg in a cast

At the Museum of Stairs

Tourists climb fleets of Penrose steps
steep as Escher's drawings
> in search of something
not knowing what
> On each level a display
gives homage to famous stairs
> the first, Loretto's Chapel
a spiral wonder that still baffles
> engineers — no visible
nails or support — this staircase
> prayed for by nuns and
nine days later
> a carpenter appeared with tools
Tourists climb not knowing the stairs
> make four 90-degree turns
in a continuous loop
> You could climb forever
and not get any higher
> Some say while ascending
a shadow races past
> a cold breath brushes the neck
and they turn to see a phantom
> Had anyone read the fine print
on their entrance ticket
> they would have known
climbing is the main attraction
> There is no visible way out
Tourists climb Escher's stairs—endlessly
climbing   climbing   climbing

THREE BEATS

Follow your inner moonlight; don't hide your madness

~Allen Ginsberg

Ginsberg and Kerouac on the Rooftop, NYC

after a photo by Ginsberg, 1953

> *evening coming—*
> *the office girl*
> *unloosing her scarf*
> ~ Jack Kerouac, haiku

Jack calls, *Ginsy boy, got a light?*
Al tosses matches. Wind douses
flame after flame. Back against
the sooted wall, Jack leans,
lichen breeds between bricks,
wind bellows in the fire escape.

> Ginsy eyes Jack's physique,
> *Is he thinking of that office girl?*

On this rooftop in search
of the *godhood of god*, Jack watches
two guys below mining a dumpster,
slides his left hand into a khaki pocket,
strokes a prized Brakeman's Manual
he found earlier in that SoHo bookstore.

Gazing the panorama, he pauses
for another long drag on a short Camel.
It takes six flicks to get it lit. Al snaps
this photo — lips pouted, Jack draws hard,
smoke grazes his roguish brow,
tangles in waves of hair.

Ferlinghetti and I on My Refrigerator
for Lawrence Ferlinghetti

It's April, poetry month. In the photo we stand squinting
in morning sun on the front lawn of Jack Webb's suburban house
where Lawrence Ferlinghetti is staying. He smiles shyly
as I wrap my arm around his shoulder. Jack snaps the photo.
I'm Larry's escort, and this afternoon he will be
the featured poet at the Border Voices Poetry Fair. But why
has he called me to pick him up so early?

When I arrived, he descended the staircase, a slim pillar of a man,
white hair, jeans, a light blue button-down and navy pull-over.
Under his arm, a trench coat, as if expecting a sudden
San Francisco gust of wind and rain in San Diego although

it's spring. After the photo, I flip my red hair,
  Larry, where would you like to go before the fair?
Gemstone blue eyes flash, he winks, *Downtown.*
Is he flirting or does he miss the cable-car city?

Yesterday on our way from the airport to Jack's
I took him on a brief San Diego tour of the Gas Lamp District,
pointed out the Horton Grand where Wyatt Earp lived.
   There's rumor of ghosts.
  Yes, downtown, he snickers, *Let's get a drink at that hotel.*
We find a booth at the Ida Bailey Pub. I order a vodka gimlet with
three green olives. He takes a craft draft. I ask,
   Have you had green olives in beer?
   Eyebrow lifted, he says, *I'll try it.*
The waitress delivers three olives that sink to the bottom
of his beer like the green of San Francisco Bay.

Salty, good, Larry says,

He tells me, how after a bypass he still rides

his bicycle over the Golden Gate bridge to Sausalito.

I'm amazed at his youthful energy, glance at my watch,

It's time for poetry

We arrive to a packed SDSU Montezuma Hall.

He takes the stage, gives a spirited reading, then ambles

over to sign books. As I wait on the sidelines, I see a flock

of young girls flirting. Three times their age, he has

charmed them with his hipster persona, his

"Coney Island of the Mind."

The next day, after taking him to the airport, Jack

stops by my home with an unexpected gift —

a bottle of Cabernet wrapped in a white doggy bag.

On the front, with his favorite black felt tip pen,

Larry has written —

for

Seretta —

This special

Napa Valley

wine

with many

thanks!

x x x

lawrence

GREEN FLASH

Life is what happens to you while you're busy
making other plans

~John Lennon

Tadpoles

On this tropical shore
ear to this shell's
chamber of sound
I hear the colloquial
voices of the sea —
the baritone of whales
squeal of dolphins
moan of manatees
menace of pirates
in pursuit of mermaids
who passed this way
long before you and I
were tadpoles
in the ocean of humanity

———————————————

lovers —
    under a blanket
        green flash sunset

Ships of Stone

In an uncharted port of the medieval past
ships were crudely carved ramparts
camouflaged by a rugged shoreline.

Visiting a dream, I wobble on precarious
high heels up a rock ledge crusted
with barnacles, pungent with moss

searching for a stone ship,
not knowing, I'm already on one
until it starts to move—

Spellbound, yet excited, I lunge
as the mammoth vessel swings
out to sea, soundless.

Climbing jagged basalt, I reach
a landing, look back to see
other stone ships in a tangle of waves.

What sea is this?

There in the twilight loom
bold mastheads of a lion,
a bear, a serpent—
ships, so hidden they're
dimly visible in the sepia fog. I feel
the heavy sway—the horrid
hush of ancient sacrifice, the tremble
of a violent seismic shift.

I sense the ominous history of bearded warriors
who honed these ships and piloted waves—
mammoth stones rising and floating like whales.

---

winter chill
the swell of waves
on this vacant beach

ochre lichen
clings to rock ledges
silent yearnings

bedrock
the volcanic eruption
we didn't see

FLESH PETALS

There is no terror in the bang, only in the anticipation of it

~Alfred Hitchcock

Mortal Things

City of poorly-loved chairs, bedroom slippers,
frying pans, I'm rushing back to you
~ Charles Simic, *Things Need Me*

A plane explodes in mid-air, colors dive like kites
plunging into a sunflower field —

cell phones drop from the summer sky
a cacophony of ringtones like mockingbirds —

frantic callers ring on and on trying to reach the fallen
strewn among yellow flowerheads —

scattered beside a red high heel
a baseball cap
a teething ring

cracked laptops hold unanswered emails
Facebook shows passenger profiles
as if nothing has happened

a gang of rebels, like raptors, raid the scene
hoard passports and credit cards,
seize black body bags
families will want returned

a wallet sprawls open —
a wedding couple
stares up at the clouds

night comes
love's scent lingers
in solitary sheets

up late writing a poem
miles away
you turn in your sleep

at dawn
the house settles
into your absence

We Didn't Do It

after Yehuda Amichai

We didn't do it in the hall of justice
nor on the cold kitchen floor.

We thought of doing it in a jet
but didn't have the nerve.

We didn't do it with fine art, delight
or clarity of mind,

didn't perspire like marathoners
pushing to the finish.

We had no fervor or conviction —
even in a catastrophe, we did nothing.

We sat — our mouths full — professed
prophets and politicians were on our side.

And when the heavens opened
it rained for nights and days —

like earth worms with no destination
we floated on the current.

How Not to Start a Summer Vacation

Police in pursuit, a driver snakes the highway,
swipes cars and a truck, broadsides,
backs up, speeds off, misses a turn.

His longbed takes on water in the bayou,
30 squad cars mass on the bridge —
rush hour traffic blocked on both sides.

Now, the fifty-something perp
is trapped, stranded in murky water.

Dark tinted glass hides his face.
The engine dies. Holding something

to his head he rolls a window down, grins,
waves at police. They wave back.

Officers wait a safe distance, he
could be carrying more guns, has
already shot at them, tossed a pistol out —

canines posed to pounce, tongues dripping.

Threats

A black flock shakes the sky.

Tell me how it feels
to be in control, to value
the surge of your breath
savor a clear mind
your faithful heart.
Take a moment to trace
the lifeforce inside you
that so quickly could be
in another's hands.

Jets rumbling — a threat only
our military knows — or not.

Monarchs, Ground Zero

after a NYC fireman's story

Search dogs guide firemen
through dense air
retched with death.

Streets sprawl, heavy laden —
walls fallen, lampposts
buried in mounds of plaster.

Mind-weary, they trudge
with hope of finding another breath.

As if called, the men look up to see
a tower of light —

a flock of Monarch butterflies
hovers and descends
through hell-born dust. One,

golden with welkin wings
comes to rest on a fireman's shoulder.
    Souls, he whispers,
    and they bow in prayer.

Hummingbird Drone

Mysterious as the manifestation
of a foreign thought
it appears in the garden
vibrating
over my left shoulder.

I don't see it at first
as the hovering winged thing
amplifies
to hear my breath and
the flutter of butterflies.

an empress Monarch
innocent as dawn
lights on the drone's metallic head
flies into a cypress followed
by a flurry of wings—

the flock rises masking the sun,
flooding a space in the lapis sky—
a host of brilliant black angels.

Under Fire

In Iraq, Chaplain Benimoff issued the troops
camouflaged   pocket-size   Bibles
indexed: loneliness   fear   duty.

Back in the US, he works at a veteran's hospital.
At night he dreams of vomiting small flag-draped
caskets, "Provider fatigue."

Back bent, hair prematurely gray,
questions of faith plague him —
> *Where have God's followers gone?*

Interviewed, he reflects,
> *Maybe it's not the brightest move*
> *to have Chaplains opening body bags to place*
> *40-pounds of ice on dead soldiers...*

> *but you have to go where your hands*
> *and heart are needed —*
> *For many months I didn't wear my cross...*
> *soldiers either run to God, holding onto*
> *who they were before, or run away*
> *from all those bombed-out-street nightmares.*

In a cold corridor he greets injured troops –
some hobbling on crutches, others limping
on prosthetics or rolling in chairs.

Once more, around his neck, a simple cross sways.
After months of loathing God and persistent prayer,
his faith has been resurrected.

> At a soldier's bedside he recites Psalms 40 —

> *I waited patiently for the Lord. He who brought me*
> *out of a horrible pit, put a new song in my mouth.*

Wounds

Gunny sips thick military coffee,
stares out the window of his trailer.
Over the lake, flushed ducks
shoot up from switchgrass.

Flashbacks jolt him — the blast —
    troops sprawled face down,
    flames sweeping, smoke, no screams.
    Ashes. Still breathing, his body quivers,
    death leaps forward, backs away
    stealing his hand.

Putting down his cup
he limps to the potter's seat,
swings one leg over,
positions a batch of wet clay,
boots the wheel.

Hunched forward he guides the lump
with his left hand and the severed stump
of his right. Clay wobbles and spins.

When the pot is formed, he places it
on the patio ledge in a line-up
with other raw vessels, shoulders a rifle,
aims, blasting the fresh pot.

The bullet cuts clean leaving
a fleshy clay petal dangling.
Sky shows through bullet holes
in the regiment of clay pots bearing
scars of violent imperfections—
wounds to be fired in a furnace,
jagged exits preserved.

pop-pop-popping
the distant sound
of target practice

slice by slice
through window blinds
thunder clouds

fish bones
in the broth
sturgeon moon

balloon man
the parrot on his shoulder
mocks shellfire

Autumn

This pine box of potpourri
holds the wrinkled skin of roses,
the ribbon and the letter you left
on my doorstep one calm autumn eve.

I can't relive love's memory
or imagine your warmth on my skin
since I outgrew that angora sweater—
a gift before you were called.

My closet holds pressed shirts —
I lean in to absorb your scent.
What was it we meant to say
that went unsaid.

If only I could gather
fallen petals from my garden,
fold them into flour, yolk and
cream to bake under a blue corn moon.

If only we could meet again
at the lake, swim like Eve and Adam
and savor petals of mooncake
before it cools.

If only you hadn't gone to war.

snow fall covers fences
boundaries vanish
strangers become lovers

funeral reception
the lid closed
on his grand piano

steep Sunset Cliffs
eroding on the edges —
a memorial bench

Critical Matter

~ for Silver

The physicist I met in Kelly's Irish Pub says
the weapons they make can't possibly
be worth the harm they cause.

He calls himself a "nuclear nerd" with a head
too big to fit through the security door
where he's called to do inspections —

says in years to come, national resources exhausted,
physicists will show the cost effective, earth-friendly
benefits of using nuclear energy for electricity.

Escorted by an armed guard, he passes through
a heavy fence. Tennis shoes squeak on the slick floor
as he enters a windowless, thick-walled room. Bushy
Einstein hair flows behind him like a wave of gray matter.

In this massive tomb where they *"do weapons"*
he sits with other "big heads" at the boardroom table.
Some sip coffee from paper cups, others inhale oxygen.

With the force to destroy everything, they believe
all we see can be formulated into cold, linear equations.
They discuss buying uranium from Russia, Canada, or
Australia, how to make "safe bombs" and keep them
from terrorists.

At the end of the day, he meets me at the Irish Pub,
orders a burger, chugs single-malt scotch, beer chasers.
Leaving a generous tip, he says the power of the *bang*
frightens him *more* than I'll ever know.

Cherry Blossom Haiku Sequence

memories of bombs
in the Japanese Park
weeping cherry trees

        Motoko's dedication
        of a friendship cherry tree
        spring memorial

                to open to close
                the memory of spring
                cherry blossom fan

wishing pond
the old frog
hoards silver coins

        pastel petals
        lit by paper lanterns
        Sakura party

                slowly
                through cherry trees
                moonlight

Valeria, Ukraine, 2022

She poses for a photo in front of blasted
bricks, rebar, glass and ashes
in her elegant gown, knowing

there will be no high school prom this year.
Gazing down at rubble, she recalls
the once green lawn at lunch hour where
she and light-hearted friends gathered.

The deep-V neckline of scarlet silk
hugs her breasts like glove to hand.
She bought it at the little boutique that is
no more, before bombs shattered her town.

Will they ever cease? Gone
to war — her father and boyfriend.
She vows to save this photo for them

and resilient generations who will
explode landmines and plant
waves of grain and sunflowers.

Ukraine Haiku Sequence

barely old enough
to shoulder a casket
Ukrainian son

Ukrainian spring
in the barren park
empty baby carriages

bomb blitz
still the pop of champagne
on New Year's Eve

Children Hear Goose-Steps

a nod to Robert Louis Stevenson

In autumn I go out to play
And wear a coat of mousy grey
I gather leaves and toss them high
Like little kites against the sky

I have to hide from brother's call
He pushes me and makes me fall
I'd like to learn to grow up fast
So I can outrun him at last

And does it not seem odd to you
When winter comes with icy dew
That we can hear men's heavy feet
Goose-stepping down our unlit street

I'd like to wear a gown of red
And light a candle by my bed
But mother tells me, *be a mouse*
All's quiet in our timorous house

RARE BLUE MOON

I'm not afraid of my own death —
I just don't want to be there when it happens

~Woody Allen

Falling

Jump, and you will find out how to
unfold your wings as you fall
　　　　　~Ray Bradbury

We find what we need in dreams of falling
anxious at first until our body accepts

gravity pulling us ever faster in a dive leading
from where we were to where we arrived.

In dreams of falling we don't see the landing,
only feel the weightless fall.

We have what we need when we awaken
to find the self who fell with us has no broken bones.

Years balance on edge. Foot-loose dreams prepare me.
I'll have what I need when I am the fallen.

———————————————————

all the dances
we couldn't do on earth
zero-gravity

Our Dead Reckoning

We apologize for killer hornets
with huge orange heads and foul deeds,
medieval in their charge of greed.

Did mankind provoke them
through our neglect?

We apologize for the rape of land,
torture of trees, pollution and debris,

apologize for the illness we have
set free through our stupidity.

Is Nature taking herself
back to Genesis
before the time of man?

Will rivers flow Sistine-Chapel-blue,
creatures rebirth harmony,
woods thrive in pure green wind?

Mother Earth, pregnant with dreams,
are you ready to begin again?

Waiting, 2019 —

We are waiting for freedom
the way we wait for word
our prisoners of war
are coming home, limbs
and lungs unscathed.

We are waiting for freedom
from fear the way we wait
for permission to hug again.
Freedom from threats will
release us from masks covering
smiles as if they could bandage fear

Fear, a blind-numbing force
spread by the massive arm
of an invisible enemy,
sweeps through the world
leaving carnage in its wake.

We wait in our homes behind closed doors,
carpets thread-bare from pacing.

———————————

new priorities
we compare notes
on shots

Pandemic Haiku Sequence

storm moon
a family of twelve
living in their car

a child breaks down
in front of schoolmates
hunger moon

Zoom viewing
the virtual reality
of a rare blue moon

perfect ending
a family picnic in the park—
pandemic masks off

Sky is our constant cloak,

holding us in place, a motherhood
of galaxy — shiny bobbles flashing
to distract us from our suffering.

One day you're young
having your turn around the sun,
but time has a way of speeding forward.
I find myself older than imagined —

a breathless hospital victim
surrounded by tubes and wires
monitoring every heartbeat.

On this night the sky holds vespers
outside the boredom of gray walls.
I glimpse a half moon and star
poised in the corner of my only window
as if placed there to give me hope.

I pretend to be well, imagine
having the strength to walk out
of this hospital into the night, to gaze up
at the sky's constant cloak, waiting
for me through the long hours of my sighs.

GHOST TWIGS

There is no line between the 'real world'
and 'world of myth and symbol.' Objects, sensations,
hit with the impact of hallucinations

~William Burroughs

Gunmetal Sky

after reading A Brief History of Time
by S. W. Hawkins

Letter found in a cave —

I could say nothing
but I care for you more than you want.

If you meet a galloping herd of feathered horses
copper mouths snapping open and shut, resist
the urge to kneel before them offering sugar.
I say this to protect you.

In this cave I welcome the hollow sound
of gunmetal sky. Before light fades, I add
one further thought to you, a question rather—
does water flow uphill in your country too?

I am writing to you from the end of this last day.
Here, stars blast holes in the sky, space
narrows. There is little for us to focus on
and we have lost sight of the wind.

Ghost Tree

In this forest a ghost tree stands,
a starched lace skeleton left by fire,
the thin trunk and fragile branches
pale against charred red cedars
with their tall voices of wind.

I will take care as I speak, breathing
with the wounded forest, breathing
with the sunlight in bare limbs,
with the flicker of remembered flames.

Puma tracks run through a dry creek
where earlier a rabbit rushed by.
When I die stand my long bones
in this cedar grove spread my fingers
like ghost twigs reaching for light.

We All Have Our Turn

In the voice of an Oracle

I write to the sound of morning awakening.
Everything desirable is somewhere
in abundance for someone. It could be you.
We all have our fleeting spins of daylight
scent of jasmine, alyssum, lilacs, the sea
a random rose blooming over
the neighbor's wall, love's enchantment
reaching into our lives, unexpected happiness.
We have our turn, all the while
unaware there's something starless —
aphids on buds, a broken wing, the candlelit
giving of last rites. Yet, if you're blessed
at this moment, seeds push tendrils
through your garden's soil, someone
is healed, small globes of sunlit lemons
lean low for gathering.
Can you avoid loneliness by savoring
solitude as it brings an awareness
not found in crowds, darkness
almost invisible until one day,
there it is, undeniable. I can't tell you
when or what it will be.
You'll know it like you know
the pulse of your life's surge
or a red storm brewing on the horizon.
I bring no stories to sadden you.
They haven't happened yet
and you're less lonely for not knowing.
Go now, gather your gems of light.

BLOOD MUSIC

…I long to lay my ear against the universe and listen
Will it too, be only the music of my own blood

~Una Nichols Hynum

A Loyal Fish

I've learned not to dread
the gaping mouth of the unknown
the lounge of a bombed airport   a sudden flash
flat-lining of my heart's final beat
My heart   a loyal fish   my breast   its ocean
the mouth a faithful
lullaby
opening
closing
life's surge
my breath
a wind
my heart
a loyal
fish

Beloved earth,

on a day much like this
the clock will make its rounds,
dawn will surrender to dusk
as my awareness seeks another place.

These fingers typing this poem
these eyes, not blind, ears tuned,
this mind, a vessel of thought—
will wander like snow.

At the heart of light
I will join a rose-flushed pigeon
in the garden of ripe tomatoes
where lizards jump for worms.

Having eluded death, for fear
of its Machiavellian ways,
I will yield to the good angel who
separates souls from cadavers.

My beloved earth, I will accede
to leaving you at that quieting hour
when awakened angels hold
afternoon sky in tired eyes.

A Zoom Meeting in Space

Following the wrong god home we may miss our star
> ~William Stafford

My virtual screen is set to outer space—
deep blue and the curve of earth
in silhouette, rim-it with galactic light.
Leaving here is a welcome calling—
no mask, no confinement, no news.
I've been muted by the stellar host.
The only sound — the distant whir
of earth tilted on axis, spinning ill-tidings
as humans attempt to adjust to "new normal."
The stars are silent, earth's energy dim.

Moment by moment a spark shoots up into space
a soul leaving earth in search of a better place.

---

    desert sky
    more stars than fit
    in my tea cup

The Mission, a Love Parable

> *It was a bright cold day in April, and the clocks*
> *were striking thirteen* ~ George Orwell

His fiancé commanded him,
    Find the world's largest clock. Smash it.
Research led to Mecca's Royal Tower, a new standard
three hours ahead of the old Jersey City Colgate clock.
She bragged to her girlfriends—

Greenwich Mean Time will soon be a blurb in history. My fiancé
    is going to prove his love by defying Universal Time.
      He'll stop the clock. We'll be forever young.

Arriving jetlagged, he took a taxi to the clock tower.
Pounding and chiseling, he entered the clock, left foot first.
Gears chewed his pant leg. He struggled,
unable to break free —

Ages shifted, flashing prayer lights blinded him. Numbers
pounded his face, dented his cheeks like the keys of an
Arabic typewriter. Pale, suddenly gray, sprawled flat
against the glass—

      shadow of the spire
      changes with time
      dawn to midnight

summer evening —
a slip of moonlight
between her thighs

a dove
folds dawn's light
to her breast

we make love
behind the sand dunes
buck moon

Canadian Geese

I never returned
to that chicken-coop on the riverbank
in India Neck
where
my son and I were poor and cold in three rooms
with a heat-giving stove,
where
we sometimes
ate mac 'n cheese for a week,
and his school lunches
were my employee meals
from the Summit House. Our
Sedan de Ville, a lover's gift, boasted
leather interior of chocolate, and when
we pulled up in front of the laundromat,
my son's pinky on a button in the glove box
made the trunk fly open.

We would unload our baskets from that classy Cadillac
into the coin-op as small-town women gossiped, their
tongues spinning slurs like the tumble of scorched jeans
in a hot drier. We were rich with our restaurant
and Dunkin' Donut friends, sparked our lives lighting
firecrackers
at Branford Point, and my
waitress tips
kept us from welfare checks. I bought
a TV and a rocking chair to establish credit. My

son played on the banks of the Connecticut River
the day his father abducted him
a third time, and I drank two bottles of cheap
wine, kept my hand on a butcher knife

beneath pillows. That cottage where
I came close to madness —
the odor of clams and lilacs at low tide,
a tire swing empty
in the snow.

Across the river trains moaned past
the wire mill where
young men's teeth corroded from chemical fumes.
I never returned to that cottage where
on the marsh I heard Canadian geese
calling to their mates.

———————————

lobsters drop
    into the boiling kettle
        squeals of summer

                    still raining
                    inside the trees
                    broken engagement

        a question posed between night-blooming jasmine

Forensics

Specks of loneliness stain the carpet,
streaks of regret stretch across
the flowered couch, memories
puddle on the kitchen floor,

a spark of sanity found in a book,
the dream of a walk in forest fog
lingers in the cluttered closet
bundled in a winter coat.

A thin hair, nearly as invisible
as a fleeting thought, clings
to a tired pandemic mask—
the villain missing.

White Jasmine creeps
through a window crack
where curtains shut out
the chatter of Spring.

On the Horizon

By night we drove, slept between states
on our marathon cross-country trek
to a custody hearing. The man I was with
had a dark side he kept hidden
but I knew at any moment it could swoop down.

He detested sunlight.
Somewhere in the south, we stopped
at a cheap motel, slept all day 'til nightfall.
I think it was Little Rock,
the humid air a wet straitjacket.

As we loaded luggage into the van
on the sidewalk in front of a boarded-up
ice cream store, a swarm of tree fogs
jumped five-feet high, their croaks magnified
in the eerie silence.

I've heard how creatures know
when a storm is coming before we do
but my thoughts were on the court verdict
and the miles ahead. We drove all night,

and on the morning news, heard
how a tornado shoveled through Little Rock
pounding the town like a gavel,
six people killed. Wind swallowed up frogs
and spit them out like rain.

Rigid

There's one on every block
and this angry boy shuts
his bedroom door to keep out
another argument in the hall,
fingers his action figure
Stretch Armstrong doll —
pliable plastic; freakishly real,
the replica of a strong man.

He tweaks its bulgy muscles, bends
the head backwards, stretches
viscous legs like rubber bands,
twists the doll's arms around its neck.

Ignoring a warning from mom
to box the doll safe from air,
he wants to feel tough, opens
the second-story window,
hurls his hero into space.
It bounces off the porch roof,
landing with a thud in devil grass.

Days later, in the garden
mother's alarmed to find
his Stretch Armstrong, rigid.
She wants to know what her son
was thinking when
he destroyed his favorite doll.

Abductor

In the hospital I lie strung up
on intravenous drips.
Death gazes through iron bars,
poses as a friend and
bribes my family. Death
reaches out to me. I extend
a tentative hand, jerk back.
Clenching smoke-stained teeth
on the frozen bars, Death's thick tongue
sticks to the window lock, its fingers
too cold to hold bright coins father offers.
mother prays, my husband lights
an eternal candle with his cigarette.
Death, blinded by the flame, shrinks
to a roach, scuttles into shadows.
The ceiling opens as I hover,
gazing down at myself, deciding
to go or stay. How tranquil to melt
into the light, but I have other lives
to consider. With a deep breath
my veins swell. Inside my womb
I feel my infant kick and turn his head.

RUMORS

standing at the blue door of a long life…
what did I come for, what was it I wanted…

Una Nichols Hynum, *The Borrower*

The Swing

The solitary swing, I see it now,
two ropes and a simple tire
hanging from an oak tree
by the path leading
to our riverbank cottage.

Wind murmurs over the grass
so softly, blades barely bend,
and the tree cradles voices
of children who once played here.

My heart sweeps to belong—

to those youthful days
when branches reached
to paint the sky cyan blue
and a boy's eyes gleamed
with promise, like pond ice.

Black n' Blue

A black De Ville appears in my rearview mirror
as I turn into the underground parking. I glance again,
recognize two men in polyester suits and shades
who visit my boss at the steakhouse where
I'm headed to work. Their order will be the usual—
steaks charred on the outside, raw in middle.

It is 1974, New Haven, Connecticut where
gang wars erupt on Chapel Street at 2 a.m.
and never make the news, and I've learned
more than I ever wanted to know.

Driving into the dead-end of echoed darkness
the De Ville follows close behind. I fear
when I leave my car, the men recognize me
in my uniform — palazzo pants, fuchsia halter.

I chill, remembering rumors other waitresses tell
about hit man Charley, and like today, he always
has a bodyguard. I've seen him stab
his Delmonico while poking fun at me, overheard
him say, *Look at her flat tits.* Yet, I admit, he tips well.

How many women become cold cases?
Every week in my mail, on the back
of a junk-flier, I see a blurred picture
of a young woman with the date she went missing
and an age-enhanced photo years later.

Seeing these men takes me back to that night
when, doors locked, we waitresses were not allowed
to go home until the streets cleared at 4 a.m.
We heard shouts and gunfire, asked no questions.

Rushing to park, I think of my son
at the YMCA nursery school waiting
for me to pick him up after work.
I dash up the ramp thankful for sunlight,
cross the street, open the heavy carved door.

In the VIP lounge city men gather for lunch—
politicians, lawyers, police, locals, mobsters
and teamsters, sip their dry "dirty martinis."
Besting each other, mouths full, they gnash
bloody black n' blue steaks.

———————————

New England summer
we stop along the roadside
buttered lobster rolls

Winter Solstice Haiku Sequence

winter solstice
horns of Pricus to the sky
hoofs to the sea

                light years away
                the Hyades star cluster
                tears apart

each flake
a quiet thought
first snow

                New Year's Eve —
                flat champagne
                distant sirens

We yield to the allure of simple things,

a swinging door, yellow walls,
an open window, light pale

as the palm of my hand
enters the room. Our cat snores,

our timeworn dog stares
through the screen at a lizard.

Happiness is a soft-serve
no matter the weather.

We play a game of rescue
where the butterfly wins.

The white owl plays
a game of mouse.

Listen. It's the simple sounds
of evening's surrender to the night.

childhood memory
the magic of making
ribbon candy

the arch
between then and now
New Year's stars

tattered mittens
my fingers warmed
where hers once were

Full Menu

When I said *yes* to this life,
I ordered from the entire menu.

Time stirred an alphabet in my soup
where I found a pinch of knowledge.
Loss dunked her tear-soaked crackers.

Bones of anger bared themselves
floating in mirky broth, swam
side strokes to get my attention.
I pushed them aside.

Regret was a tough steak
I wanted to send back,
hungry for substance,
peeved I'd made poor choices.

Compassion, a sweet compote,
arrived at my table.
I savored each spoonful
like a child in an ice cream parlor.

DANDELION WINE

Who has not sat before his own heart's curtain?
It lifts and the scenery is falling apart.

~Rainer Maria Rilke

First Connecticut Winter

The first time I saw snow on the beach
I strolled with my son's gentle dog, Mindy.
We made footprints in powder, crunched
dense crust like the first moonwalkers.

That quiescent night, slabs of ice creaked
in the Long Island Sound, holding back waves
like tectonic plates when a tremor
kicks the planet—waves too far away to hear.

Our lives trembled on the faulted edge of change—

As we walked, dark trees lurked like tall men
in eerie silence, about to give verdicts
I didn't want to hear. Porch lights flowed
over our path casting slippery silhouettes.

This California winter night, sand holds warmth
long after sunset where Pacific waves roar
three thousand miles from the Atlantic Ocean.
Mindy's shadow walks beside me.

Some Things Are Better Left Behind

in memory of G. Cabral, 1967-1985

Summer is here,
though there's no soft-shelled crab,
no buttered lobster rolls at roadside stands
as in New England—
no scent of lilacs blooming in our yard,
no dandelion salad from the riverbank where sun
shone through the lace of trees, and blossoms
drifted in swirls on the river's flow.

Summer is here in the dry foothills of California
though the dessert wind hasn't arrived
to prompt blooms in our cactus garden,
the palm-lined creek is full of pollywogs, and
my son walks his old dog, Sugar, as he did Mindy
in that small Victorian town, her lifetime ago.

His memories teeter-totter forward and back,
but he vows not to return to that overgrown
griffin's garden where he and his childhood friend
played hide 'n seek, where sun never reached
their favorite shade and the remains of a rope
may still dangle from the tree where
his buddy was cut down.

Waking in Winter

My love, asleep in our warm bed,
silver curls flowing on your pillow—
may your sleep be blissful,
may your dreams be sensual, may you
awaken lighthearted.

A winter storm roars around our home,
and the call just came—
my hospice patient, younger than
you and I, died last night.

Letters I wrote for her
will surely be read time and again.
The first, to grandchildren—
lavish praise, abundant with
      I love you

A reluctant messenger, I delivered
the second letter to her husband—
      You must let me go
And a few days later, in a quiet breeze
from her open window, she was gone.

My love, here we are in our winter nest
this eleventh month together.
Let us embrace like the blankets
hugging us from toe to chin.

Arrival

Summer arrives swishing her sheer
skirt, hair flung wild by Santa Anna wind.
I forgive her hot breath willing
African daisies to wither. I thank her
for calling the sunset epiphyllum
to a glorious magenta-orange bloom.

Shamrock weeps the loss of spring.
My love and I reach for our phones,
text each other at the same time
feeling the cool, as evening invites us
to stroll through this solstice awakening —
our steps slower with age as we climb
a steep hill, pausing part way for a hug.

Who dressed summer in her day-bright colors,
who will dress her in a gown of night stars,
and dangle planets like beads around her neck.

---

    planets held deep
    in a yellow trumpet flower
    cosmic coitus

super moon
coming through the keyhole
summer visitor

toddler tide-pooling
even the bubbles
surprise her

a narrow place
between wings
winter moonlight

Dandelion Wine

I awaken not knowing the time. Color is gone
from a vacant space in the sky where spinnakers blew,
sailors turn back to shore.
            Is it late afternoon?

My breath is hot dust on a bedside water glass.
Outside, gray flattens tree shapes, confounds the hour.
            Is it dawn,
have I missed our sips at sunset?

A woman can't sleep in a room full of questions,
she needs to know when comfort will come.

I search the room in a daze,
afloat in the haze of an uncertain hour,
            awaiting your return
and our nips of dandelion wine.

---

            morning after
            her little black dress sways
            on the clothesline

Summer Haiku Sequence

summer shoreline
dots follow dashes—
fleeting sandpipers

visiting the beach
where I was young
green sea glass

swiped by a seagull
the toddler's
bag of chips

summer shoreline
chased by *terrible twos*
a nervous seagull

curled plump commas
punctuate a sand-line
harbor seals

the ocean starfish in starlight

OVERTAKING GLASS

…And above the dark trees a window is always lit,
in memory of the face that looked out of it, and that
face too was in memory of another lit window.

~Yehuda Amichai, *Eternal Window*

Those We Lose

after "In Blackwater Woods" by Mary Oliver

Things I've learned in life lead back to this—
the dark eyes of loss whose other side is want.

Today I trim jasmine and plant new clippings
as a flash of memory arrives — the lover
who died this year three thousand miles away—

buried in that small town cemetery
where we took photos of stones worn faceless
by time's indifference.

On country rides we stopped at cemeteries,
meandered through headstones remarking
on names, dates and those with none.

Blue arms of sky embrace evergreens.
In my garden I feel the heat of his presence,
feel the intensity of his jet eyes on me.

If I make the trip again, to that place where
we met, I'll find his bones waiting.

---

after the funeral
in an intimate dream
his familiar touch

Connecticut Woods

Leaves crackle under footsteps
in the dense silhouette of trees

syncopation of sounds   din of millions
cackle of crickets   froth of frogs

cacophony

millions of flecks   prowl branches
a sturgeon moon reveals   millions of eyes

in the dense silhouette of trees

this symphony of sound   engulfing me
will carry on   long after
I am less than a shadow

another speck

Night Blinks, Sleeping on the River

Out through birch woods
    down the gravel road we amble
        out to a solitary dock on the river
where we praise the design of stars—
    out to where midnight wears a gauzy robe
        and silence breathes
            like sleeping shore birds.
We arrive at your boat
    slip off our cotton clothes—
        listen to the rocking of our narrow bed
rising and falling with cricket calls.
    Night blinks. Sleeping on the river
        summer's breath in our ears
            and on our lips—
    we turn to each other
        wrapping our arms
            around youth.

A Clock of Songbirds

Before you know what love is
you must dance in the rain
promising seven happy moments
to the thief in your kitchen, burn
a candle for someone you've never met.

Before you know what love is
you must piece together threadbare
memories of a lover who disappeared.

Take a moment to wonder why
some lovers hurry to believe, hurry
to tie a double knot in the strings of desire,
and others refrain.

You must take the deepest sorrow
from your neighbor
and give a clock of songbirds
set to the hand of dawn.

Love's gravity opens the sky —
a space quivers between branches.
Under the wolf moon, in the solitude
of your heart, listen to a white owl's call
until you know.

Seaweed in My Stilettos

By the bay window at the Marine Room
we stayed late watching the candelabra burn.

Sallow wax pooled on white linen,
wind whirled pine boughs; thunder snapped
lightning lit turbulent waves like a horror film.

Our waiter warned us before he went home.
I squeezed your thigh when a wall of water
threatened windows.

Night advanced as we drank rain, dined
on wind, hailed ocean overtaking glass.

When the restaurant filled ankle-deep,
seaweed twined around my lime green stilettos —
        our lips met as your tie floated neck high.

Ethereal

inspired by Daniel Camp paintings

Walking out of the morning fog
a woman's hand appears
holding the sash of her red gown.
Her stockings black, red seams
up the back, define the speed of her gait —
a sashay, as if tipsy entering a stage.

Steamed car windows
blur my vision. The day is cold.
Rain specks my windshield
in drops the size of a dime
for yesteryear's phone call.

This woman could be on her way
home after a one-night-stand,
which explains no coat.
Is she a femme fatale
from a romance novel?

The rain has stopped.
Bare limbs of a liquid amber
loom sinister; a few leaves cling.
I pull over to offer her a ride,
roll down the window —
the fog, ethereal, and so is she.

Glass House of Steam

I want to awaken nude by your side
in this glass house—

the quiet frame and transparent walls
absorbing, reflecting

body warmth, aroma of jasmine tea—
white buds bursting in steam.

I want to awaken nude by your side
and we won't mind the squirrels
            pausing
                from time to time
                    for a quick peek.

Sweet Trill

A pair of doves flies to the roof top, hop around,
flit away with that sweet trill only they know.
I think to myself, that's their roof,

one of many they own a few moments a day
like the moon owns the stars, the sun owns
the sky, then rain owns, and then, and then,

each dove's concern is the other, that's all.
Life is good in the simple dove world.
More often at this age, I think to myself, I'm

content to watch the dove-couple coupling,
their dart of wings, spirit of dancing feet,
while my blind house cat sleeps so close, I feel

the vibration of her breath, her snore pacing
the approach of night, the throb of our old hearts.

To the Curtain at the Window

Let the early morning rain
patter prancing footsteps
up the stairs. Let passion flowers sip.

Let the rain gauge fill to the brim
as a snail makes its journey
tracking labored time.

Let rust cling to the keys lost
in dry leaves. Let wind tug
on the rope, calling a bell to song.

Let the lover alone in bed find
relief from stress and yearning
in the comfort of a dream.

Let the apples in the garden
fill with juice and shine.
Let sun in. Let worms come.

To the curtain at the window,
to the watch on the wrist. To breath
in the lung. Let sun come.

Let it warm, as it will, and rest
assured, change captures all.
So let sun in, let in the rain.

Winged Morning

Bird gossip, the only voices I hear
this cool morning—
winged, unsettled
these words arrive on the page.
They have lingered in the clouds
around the cypress searching
seeking a surface to touch
a reason to be —
to be placed next to other words
to reach for meanings
as plaintive as the low pitch
of a mourning dove.
The writer sits in an easy chair asking
the words what they want to say.
Some agree to speak, others choose
to perch outside the window
in a distant pine, wanting
to be left alone.
A crow's interruption cuts silence
sweeps a figurative wing across the page
leaving a cackle in its wake.
Another flock of words have flown in
wanting to speak.

Holograms

In the presence of light
time and flesh no longer matter,
no body to nurture, no urgent needs,

only freedom to merge with rays of light,
and air — the ethereal place where you see
the deceased — alive and young.

You want to reach through light to touch.
This feeling lingers in shadows before dawn.

ACKNOWLEDGMENTS

My grateful appreciation to the following publications
in which some of these poems appeared in earlier versions:

Serving House Journal

Margie, The American Journal of Poetry

Oberon Foundation Journal

City Works Press anthology

California Quarterly

The California State Poetry Society

Muse Apprentice Guild, International Literary Review

Waymark, Voices of the Valley

Weave Journal

Poppyseed Kolache Anthology (MaryAnka Press)

California Climate and Water; A Change Crisis Anthology

A Year in Ink anthologies (Ink Spot Press)

Oasis Journals (Imago Press)

Moonday Poets

Visions (Mind, Body, Spirit, Earth) Magazine

Magee Park Poets anthologies

Tidepools, A Journal of Ideas

San Diego Poetry Annual (Garden Oak Press)

Best of Border Voices (Level4 Press)

Border Voices Poetry Project anthologies

California Poets in the School anthologies

San Diego Writer's Monthly

Poetic Voices

St. Mark's Annual Art Festival

San Gabriel Valley Poetry Quarterly

UK Newspaper (Russian translations)

HAIKU PUBLICATIONS

Modern Haiku anthology

Frogpond, Journal of the Haiku Society of America

Contemporary Haibun Online

Hedgerow, a journal of small poems,

Under the Basho

Brass Bell, a haiku journal

Troutswirl, THF Blog The Haiku Foundation

Poetry Pea journal of haiku and senryu

Shaping Water: Erotic Haiku & Tanka (Moth Orchid Press)

Seabeck anthology, Haiku Pacific Rim anthology

Southern California Haiku Study Group anthologies

Inkscrawl (Stone Bird Press)

failed haiku, a journal of English senryu.

bottle rockets

Haiku Down Under anthology

Several of the poems in this volume were selected from Seretta's book, *Foreign Dust Familiar Rain,* a limited edition of her poetry and illustrations. Special thanks to Marion Martin Dickes, Una Nichols Hynum, Fred Longworth and Megan Webster for their fine editing of that book. A bow to Jane Hirshfield for her inspiration and the words "foreign dust" from her poem, *Envoy.* Seretta thanks the following people and institutions, whose support was invaluable —
The James Irvine Foundation, Poets and Writers, Poetry International Journal, The Linda Brown Scholarship, and the generous support of Sandra Alcosser, Ilya Kaminsky, Katie Farris, Kate Gale, Suzanne Lummis, Steve Kowit, Diane Wakoski, Fred Longworth and Clifton King whose patient, abiding enthusiasm made this book a reality. Deep gratitude to fellow-teachers of The Border Voices Poetry Project, the founding director Jack Webb, and the California Poets in the Schools. Heartfelt appreciation to a host of other poets including Ellen Bass, LoVerne Brown Poetry Circle, Live Oaks, Blue Stockings, Oasis Learning Center and the Idyllwild Poetry and Arts community.

NOTES ON THE POEMS

Akashic Records   *Intro page*

In the religion of Theosophy and the spiritual movement called
Anthroposophy, the **Akashic records** are a compendium of all
universal events, thoughts, words, emotions, and intent ever to
have occurred in the past, present, or future in terms of all entities
and life forms, not just human. They are believed by theosophists to
be encoded in a non-physical plane of existence known as the
mental plane. Because it is believed that the records are encoded
vibrationally into the inherent fabric of space, some have likened
the mechanism to how **holograms** are created.

At the Comic-Con of the Future   11

haibun dedicated to the San Diegans who founded Comic-Con in
1970 —Shel Dorf, Richard Alf, Ken Krueger, Ron Graf, and Mike
Towry and those dedicated workers who serve at this yearly event.

Silent Film Theater,   *9, 11 ,72*
At the Comicon of the Future,
The Mission, A Love Parable

These haibun are a Japanese genre of writing that marries prose
with haiku. The prose part typically describes a setting, scene, or
moment in an objective manner following haiku considerations,
and the haiku is in juxtaposition to and punctuates the prose.

Ode to Marc Chagall   13

Dedicated to my cousin, Rosalind who viewed the exhibition with
me. This poem addresses many paintings but at the end of the
poem it focuses on his painting, "The Elusive. "

Museum of Stairs   19

Inspired by the artist, M. C. Escher's most famous lithograph,
"Reality," depicting a complex architectural structure show
people walking upside down and sideways. The paradoxical
Penrose staircase takes form when the brain attempts to turn a 2D

image into a 3D object. From years of trusted experience, our minds assume lines are always straight and corners precisely 90 degrees. But those facts can't be true and still create this eternal four-way staircase.

40   *Monarchs, Ground Zero, Under Fire*
A true account from a magazine of what firemen at Ground Zero experienced and told a journalist.

43   *Wounds*
After meeting a Vietnam veteran who made clay pots on a potter's wheel, then shot a hole through each one. The finished pots had what the poem describes as "fleshy petals" where the bullet exploded through the neck of the pot. He lived at Lake Otay, Chula Vista, California, in a trailer and worked as a Concessioners.

48, 50, 58, 86, 99   *Haiku Sequences*
A succession of haiku which often have a narrative thread and are all on a theme, having some creative constraints or central idea linking the haiku. Each haiku can be three lines, two lines or one line (monoku).

69   *A Loyal Fish*
    The poet's response to watching an EKG monitor her heart.

107   *Seaweed in My Stilettos*
Fantasy. The Marine Room is a historical fine dining seafood restaurant in La Jolla, Ca., established in 1941, and repaired many times due to ocean damage.

109   *Glass House of Steam*
After visiting Philip Johnson's "Glass House," New Canaan, Ct.

About the Author

Holographic Reality, Poems of an Eclectic Life is Seretta Martin's most recent book. As the managing editor of the San Diego Poetry Annual, Seretta hosts annual publication readings. She has been a finalist for the *Philip Levine Prize, The Washington Prize,* and *Atlanta Review.* Awards include the *Poets and Writers, the James Irvine Foundation, The California Quarterly.* Her work has been published over twenty-five years in America and the United Kingdom and her book reviews have appeared on *Web del Sol, Poetry International* and *Synesthesia Journal.* Often her poetry appears in *The Haiku Foundation Blog; Troutswirl, frogpond, Modern Haiku, A Year in Ink, San Diego Poetry Annual, Border Voices Poetry Project anthologies,* and *The Southern California Haiku Study Group anthologies.* Border Voices Poetry in the Schools interviews can be viewed on the ITV archives. She is a co-founder of Haiku San Diego and Synesthesia Literary Journal. At Barnes and Noble she founded New Alchemy Poetry, a thirteen-year series. Born during a blizzard at Saint Mary's Hospital, Illinois, and raised in San Diego, California, Seretta received her MFA in English and a BS in Television, Video, Film and Educational Technology from San Diego State University. Previously, she studied visual arts at Madam Chouinard's and Walt Disney's art and music school, Chouinard Art Institute, Los Angeles. After Disney's death the school became California Institute of the Arts, Valencia, Ca. She recalls "the luscious smell of paint lockers in that old art deco school a few blocks from MacArthur Park—famously known for 1960's political rallies, romantic Sunday boat rides, and the inspiration for the classical music composition, *MacArthur Park.*" Seretta has taught over twenty years in her hometown of San Diego, and lives in the peaceful foothills away from the maddening crowds of "American's Finest City."

Poetry is an orphan of silence. The words never quite equal
the experience behind them.

~Charles Simic

The work of the eyes is done. Go now and do the heart-work
on the images imprisoned within you

~Rainer Maria Rilke

Made in the USA
Monee, IL
18 September 2024

65504917R00090